Yoga Exercises for Teens

Ordering

Trade bookstores in the U.S. and Canada please contact:

Publishers Group West
1700 Fourth St., Berkeley CA 94710
Phone: (800) 788-3123   Fax: (800) 351-5073

Hunter House books are available at bulk discounts for textbook course adoptions;
to qualifying community, health-care, and government organizations;
and for special promotions and fund-raising. For details please contact:

Special Sales Department
Hunter House Inc., PO Box 2914, Alameda CA 94501-0914
Phone: (510) 865-5282   Fax: (510) 865-4295
E-mail: ordering@hunterhouse.com

Individuals can order our books from most bookstores,
by calling **(800) 266-5592**, or from our website at
www.hunterhouse.com

Yoga Exercises for Teens

Developing a Calmer Mind and a Stronger Body

Helen Purperhart

Translated by Amina Marix Evans
Illustrated by Barbara van Amelsfort

Hunter House
PUBLISHERS

Copyright © 2009 Uitgeverij Panta Rhei, Katwijk
Illustrations © Barbara van Amelsfort
First published in the Netherlands in 2005 by Panta Rhei
as *Het yoga avontuur voor jongeren.*
Clipart © 2008 Jupiterimages Corporation

Hunter House Inc., Publishers
PO Box 2914
Alameda CA 94501-0914

Library of Congress Cataloging-in-Publication Data

Purperhart, Helen.
[Yoga avontuur voor jongeren. English]
Yoga exercises for teens : developing a calmer mind and a stronger body /
Helen Purperhart ; translated by Amina Marix Evans ; illustrated by
Barbara van Amelsfort. – 1st ed.
p. cm. – (A Hunter House Smartfun book)
Includes bibliographical references and index.
ISBN-13: 978-0-89793-503-6 (pbk.)
ISBN-10: 0-89793-503-9 (pbk.)
ISBN-13: 978-0-89793-504-3 (spiral bound)
ISBN-10: 0-89793-504-7 (spiral bound)
1. Hatha yoga for teenagers.   2. Physical fitness for youth.
3. Teenagers–Health and hygiene.   I. Title.
RA781.7.P88413 2008
613.7'0460835–dc22   2008024262

Project Credits

Cover Design: Jil Weil & Stefanie Gold
Illustrations: Barbara van Amelsfort
Translator: Amina Marix Evans
Book Production: John McKercher
Developmental and
Copy Editor: Amy Bauman
Proofreader: Herman Leung
Acquisitions Editor: Barbara Moulton
Editor: Alexandra Mummery
Senior Marketing Associate: Reina Santana

Production Assistant: Amy Hagelin
Editorial Intern: Kimberley Merriss
Publicity Intern: Sean Harvey
Rights Coordinator: Candace Groskreutz
Customer Service Manager:
   Christina Sverdrup
Order Fulfillment: Washul Lakdhon
Administrator: Theresa Nelson
Computer Support: Peter Eichelberger
Publisher: Kiran S. Rana

Printed and Bound by Bang Printing, Brainerd, Minnesota

Manufactured in the United States of America

9 8 7 6 5 4 3 2 1   First Edition   08 09 10 11 12

SmartFun Activity Books from Hunter House

101 Music Games for Children by Jerry Storms

101 More Music Games for Children by Jerry Storms

101 Dance Games for Children by Paul Rooyackers

101 More Dance Games for Children by Paul Rooyackers

101 Movement Games for Children by Huberta Wiertsema

101 Drama Games for Children by Paul Rooyackers

101 More Drama Games for Children by Paul Rooyackers

101 Improv Games for Children by Bob Bedore

101 Language Games for Children by Paul Rooyackers

101 Life Skills Games for Children by Bernie Badegruber

101 More Life Skills Games for Children by Bernie Badegruber

101 Cool Pool Games for Children by Kim Rodomista

101 Family Vacation Games by Shando Varda

101 Relaxation Games for Children by Allison Bartl

101 Pep-Up Games for Children by Allison Bartl

101 Quick-Thinking Games + Riddles for Children by Allison Bartl

404 Deskside Activities for Energetic Kids by Barbara Davis, MA, MFA

Yoga Games for Children by Danielle Bersma and Marjoke Visscher

The Yoga Adventure for Children by Helen Purperhart

The Yoga Zoo Adventure by Helen Purperhart

Yoga Exercises for Teens by Helen Purperhart

Important Note

The material in this book is intended to provide information about a safe, enjoyable exercise program for teenagers. Every effort has been made to provide accurate and dependable information. The contents of this book have been compiled through professional research and in consultation with professionals. However, professionals have differing opinions, and some of the information may become outdated; therefore, the publisher, authors, and editors, as well as the professionals quoted in the book cannot be held responsible for any error, omission, or dated material. The authors and publisher assume no responsibility for any outcome of applying the information in this book. Follow the instructions closely. Note that teenagers' bodies differ, and no one should be forced to assume any physical positions that causes them pain or discomfort. If you have questions concerning your exercise program or the application of the information described in this book, please consult a qualified yoga professional.

Contents

*A detailed list of the games indicating
appropriate group sizes begins on the next page.*

*Please note that the illustrations in this book are all outline drawings.
The fact that the pages are white does not imply that the people all have
white skin. This book is for people of all races and ethnic identities.*

List of Exercises

Foreword

Her wild hair danced in the sun as we did the workshop. It is always a pleasure for me to go out with her, have fun together, discover new things, and be creative together. During the four years I have been working with Helen on a regular basis, we have each grown in our own ways. I truly believe that it is a gift if you can share, discuss, and assimilate experiences with a like-minded person. In life, every person has her own journey toward a certain goal. In all of our meetings we have discovered how important this is. The interesting thing is that our generation is only just discovering this kind of wisdom in adulthood; ideally we should be gaining such insight—about our bodies and about life in general—when we are young. That would give us so much more time to develop an awareness of our bodies and learn how to relax them.

Fortunately, current developments in the world of yoga—which encourage participation by children and teens—allow us to put some of that wisdom into practice. And just in time, too. Raising children both at home and in the broader community is becoming ever-more challenging and many young people are simply desperate for help in getting in touch with their bodies.

Helen and I play a wonderful yoga game with the children when we are invited to a primary school. It is rewarding to watch the children become so animated by the simplest of exercises; as soon as children become aware of themselves, their eyes start to sparkle. By playing yoga games with children, we can teach them to love themselves. And, at the same time, they become a mirror for us should we take ourselves too seriously. In fact, it goes without saying that everyone can become a child again. That is why it is important that children do not get left behind; we need to help them realize that there is so much more to life than just "hanging about." As well, they need to remember that treating each other with respect and caring for and about each other is normal, and that it is fun and entertaining to listen to each other.

Helen's gift lies in the fact that she has great insight into working with young people. And one insight she has, as she points out in this book, is that yoga has so much to offer young people. It can be done either alone or in groups. It gives students great satisfaction: They discover that even though they are young, they are able to solve problems and feel strongly about things. Finally, just working with the body can be both enlightening and exhilarating. Helen tries to make all of this apparent in the numerous examples and approaches she gives in the exercises. I have Helen to thank for a journey through the world of movement. Yoga and painting are not the only workshops we attend; she takes me to all kinds of other workshops. And in attending these workshops we experience the same things as the children and adults who come to us for a workshop: relaxation, insight, and love for yourself.

The best thing we can teach each other is to care for each other and to love yourself, so that we can pass this on to other people.

We dance on and are not afraid of making mistakes or of having to say "I'm sorry."

We remain open-minded and see our families growing along with us. We show that we are women, strong and flexible.

Helen, thank you for being my friend, and let us always remember to be children.

– Emeke Buitelaar

Preface

A Little Bit about My Story

I had my first experience with yoga when I was a child. I remember thinking it was a pretty strange thing to do—lying on a mat, making contact with the floor. It all seemed rather silly to me. In addition, I missed the connection with my peer group as it was a class for adults. After that experience I had nothing more to do with yoga for many years.

When I became pregnant in 1992 I joined a pregnancy yoga class. I discovered how I could help myself unwind through relaxation exercises and meditation. As I became more involved with yoga I thought, "This is it!" so I quickly decided to take a course in order to become a yoga teacher. Everything I had learned up until that point was covered in the course.

Since I had been a youth worker and civics teacher, from the very beginning I knew I wanted to work with young people. When I became a yoga teacher, I began giving yoga lessons to the children at a school for students with learning problems in Amsterdam. I have been working there for over twelve years now. Initially, remembering my own early yoga experiences, I thought that it would be hard to motivate these "difficult" children to do yoga. At first, they did snicker and giggle a lot, and it took them time to get used to the exercises, sitting still, and gaining control over their thoughts. But to my amazement, they came away from the classes more relaxed and with very positive attitudes about the experience. Yoga has now become a hugely important part of the school's curriculum, and the children sign up voluntarily.

When I set out on my spiritual journey, I did not see it as a search for enlightenment. I was primarily looking for rest, tranquility, and control over my thoughts. But the farther I went along the path of yoga, the more interested I became in living more consciously. I felt and experienced that I was connected with everyone and everything, and it was a wonderful feeling. For example, in raising my two daughters—Nina is eleven and Carmel is four—I recognize myself in them over and over again. It can even be disturbing because, for example, I recognize that they have not learned a particular negative or inappropriate behavior from a stranger. But the more aware I become of the interaction between people, the closer and closer I come to finding answers to my own life questions.

Since 2000, apart from my role as a mother, I also have taken on that of the head of the children's yoga center, Jip and Jan, in Almere, the Netherlands. There, and in other parts of the country, I give yoga classes for children, teenagers, and adults, as well as courses about children's yoga to group leaders and yoga teachers. In the Foreword you met Emeke Buitelaar. I have discovered wonderful qualities in her that I now realize I have as well but had forgotten about. We embarked on a profound, if willful, alliance and continue to learn a great deal from each other. In addition to children's yoga, we also lead dance and theater workshops and regularly give electrifying dance performances at schools and businesses. I further channel my passion for yoga into writing about it—hopefully to the benefit of others on similar journeys. I now have a number of books besides this one, including *The Yoga Adventure for Children* and *The Yoga Zoo Adventure*, both of which are also published by Hunter House.

About This Book

Currently, not many yoga classes are offered specifically for teenagers. Although yoga teachers find this an interesting target group, they will more often than not invite a young person to join an adult group. But young people, I think, find it far nicer to perform yoga in a group of their peers, and since people were constantly asking me for suggestions for yoga lessons for this age group, I decided that it would be simpler to write a book on the subject. The resulting book—*Yoga Exercises for Teens*—is intended to help young people become more aware of their bodies and learn ways to relax. Yoga, as the book shows, is a positive way for teenagers to deal with all the changes that their bodies and minds are going through during this period of life.

This is a practical book; anyone who works with teens can use the postures and exercises it presents without a huge amount of preparation. More experienced yoga teachers will also find it useful as they can use the ideas to craft lessons in their own style. Certainly the possibilities shown here are not the only ways to do things, so be creative.

In the first few sections of the book I speak about the yoga life rules, which lie at the basis of all forms of yoga. I then give a number of practical tips for teaching yoga to teens. I have also included the results of an academic study carried out by Sanna Maris, which form the basis of this workbook. Sanna Maris graduated in pedagogy from the University of Utrecht in 2004. She researched the influence of yoga on problem teenagers at a school in Amsterdam. She did the same with a group of teenagers who took yoga classes at a neighborhood center in Rotterdam.

In the book's later sections, we describe the exercises that will help young people develop a better awareness of their bodies. The breathing exercises will teach them to observe their breathing patterns. They will become aware of how they feel and the ways in which they breathe. They will discover their bodies so that they become more aware and will be able to avoid or reduce stress. The stretching exercises serve as preparation for the yoga exercises and also for cooling down to rest the body after exertion.

The exercises offer a relaxed and pleasurable way for young people to work on their bodies and minds. The yoga exercises are divided into *static postures* that are mainly about concentration and power, *dynamic postures* that coordinate body movements and breathing, *relaxation postures* to bring the body to rest, and *partner exercises* that emphasize working in pairs.

The final section of the book presents *visualization exercises*. These exercises take teens on guided imaginary adventures of discovery in their minds. The students are then brought back to the here and now with special wake-up exercises.

Acknowledgments

Learning is discovering what you already know....

Dorothy L. – *Chicken Soup for the Soul*

I dedicate this book to my dear and patient husband, Marc Leeser, who always helps me to follow my path. I thank him for the support we find together as parents. I dedicate it also to my daughters, Nina and Carmel, the mirrors through which I gain insight into myself and learn to understand others better. Many thanks to Sanna Maris for allowing me to use excerpts from her research. It was great to work together in the yoga classes at the VSO-ZMOK school in Amsterdam. My thanks go also to Sophie van der Zee, Marion Gravendaal, and Leonieke and Elly de Wildt-Dienske, all of whom gave me positive feedback during the making of this book. Thanks to Emeke Buitelaar for writing the Foreword and for the wonderful adventures we have together. I thank Barbara van Amelsfort, with whom it has been such a pleasure to work, for her wonderful illustrations that make this book what it has become. In addition, my thanks go to all the students to whom I have taught yoga; you have all been my teachers.

Information
for the
Teacher

Yoga and the Search for Balance

In their teens, young people explore and discover themselves and search for their identity. They long to be themselves and to take control of themselves and their lives. It is a period during which they have conflicts with their parents, teachers, and others about music, clothes, and rules. Gradually, their relationships with parents and educators move toward equality. At the same time, young people turn enthusiastically to the outside world. Full of self-confidence, they jump into adventures, spending more and more time away from home in order to get to know the world, to form friendships and other personal relationships, and to make important choices.

Many young people experience this phase of their life as a chaotic period of recognition, denial, sadness, and pleasure. Socially it is hard; they try to understand how society fits together as they watch the ways in which people deal with each other. Some teens feel insecure because they think they ought to look or behave in a certain way. Others test how it is to respond to situations and experiences drawing on their own thoughts and feelings. Some wrestle with divided emotions, feeling that they are not living up to their parents' and peers' expectations and also knowing deep down that they are not living up to their own, either. Fitting in, acceptance, joining in, and rejection all play a hugely important role at this time. And even when young people think they've "made it"—that they have it figured out—they still have anxieties about letting go of the familiar world of their parents, the family home, and their childhood. It confuses them to feel so grown up and yet know that they still need guidance because they don't yet understand it all.

This is also a difficult period for many teens because young people are often uncomfortable with themselves. They find it hard to concentrate, to do their homework, and to feel good about themselves. In addition, they have a lot to deal with. Not only are they expected to perform well at school (where important exams will influence their future careers), but they have a huge amount of information and many choices thrown at them on a daily basis. They can watch TV all day long, go on the Internet, play computer games, or send and receive e-mail. Some young people have no problem handling such a busy life, but many of them simply cannot deal with it. Many young people, confronted with all the distractions of an ever-busier society, lose sight of their goals. And through all of this stress, they lose contact with their physical selves.

The stress of all of this can manifest itself in many ways—from physical disorders to a negative self-image. Symptoms such as bad moods, restlessness, and headaches or stomach aches with no clear cause frequently occur during this period. Some young people may become listless and dependent; others exhibit challenging behavior or are constantly plagued by a stream of disturbing thoughts and/or irritations that they can't let go of but that tire them out. The more difficult it becomes for them to shut themselves off from all the stimuli, the more they start to lose touch with their bodies. It is therefore very important that young people become more aware of themselves, life's many outside influences, and the world in which they live.

Yoga can be a good tool for dealing with this age and these matters. Some young people come to yoga interested only in the pleasure and relaxation aspects; others seek yoga's more spiritual aspects. In general, all find it interesting to discover themselves and fascinating to come to an understanding of how much their thoughts and actions influence their lives. Of course, the depth of yoga's influence and what a young person gains from its practice varies from one individual to another.

The Yoga Rules of Life

Yoga had already existed for a couple of thousand years before we began counting. The word *yoga* means "binding"; you bind the physical, mental, and spiritual elements of your life. Body and mind were seen as a single unit. Human beings are connected with all things on the planet—whether people, animals, plants, earth, air, or water. Yoga meditation techniques and methods for living a healthier life grew out of this viewpoint.

These teachings are found in traditional yoga scriptures, which were written in the ancient Indian language of Sanskrit. The scriptures consist of short texts outlining the essence of yoga, and the best known of these texts were written by the ancient teacher Patanjali. He describes the "eight-fold path" of yoga as:

1. *yama*—the five abstinences designed for avoiding bad habits (moral principles)
2. *niyama*—the five good habits (personal disciplines)
3. *asana*—attaining physical health, strength, and flexibility through the practice of physical postures (yoga postures/positions)
4. *pranayama*—controlling energy through breathing for the attainment of added vitality (yoga breathing)
5. *pratyahara*—focusing attention within for the preservation of emotional peace (withdrawal of senses)
6. *dharana*—concentrating attention on a particular spot as a way to increase mental power (concentration)
7. *dhyana*—eliminating disturbing thoughts during concentration so that you can achieve meditation (meditation)
8. *samadhi*—state of bliss resulting from a merge with the universal consciousness; realization of pure consciousness (union)

The first two aspects of yoga are concerned with respect for yourself, your surroundings, and society as a whole. The other aspects of yoga bring about the first processes of physical awareness and concentration. Yoga is currently practiced in a number of different ways. In both the East and the West many schools of yoga interpret yoga in their own way. This book makes no attempt to provide a complete picture of the classical system of yoga; it is a step on the path toward greater awareness of body and mind.

The Five Abstinences

The first of the rules of yoga concerns abstinence. You abstain from all kinds of bad habits including violence, lying, theft, and desire. These are universal moral commandments concerning the outer world.

1. Nonviolence

The *first abstinence* is the development of a nonviolent attitude toward life. Through this abstinence, young people can learn to recognize their anger, aggression, and ignorance; to experience it consciously; and to accept it. By asking young people to examine what makes them angry, they can create a distance between themselves and whatever makes them feel that way. Acceptance creates the possibility for change and allows people to become more loving. Once a young person is no longer hostage to aggression, preconceptions, and a suspicious nature, he or she will be able to create an attitude free of violence.

2. Truth and Honesty

The *second abstinence* is about speaking the truth and conducting yourself accordingly. Adults can encourage young people to be truthful by talking to them about lying and its consequences. Praise them if they act and speak honestly without insulting or making a fool of someone else. Speaking the truth gives a person more self-assurance; it also helps gain other people's trust. When discussing this issue with teens, pose the following dilemma to generate a discussion:

> Imagine that your best friend is being sought by the police. Officers come to your house and ask if you know this person, whether you have seen him, and if you know where he is. Will you tell the truth in this case?

3. Not Stealing

The *third abstinence* is about not taking anything that does not belong to you. This doesn't refer to just the theft of objects, but also to the stealing of other people's ideas. Encourage young people to use their own original ideas. They can discuss the results of stealing on themselves and the repercussions for the victims. Try the following dilemmas for them to discuss:

- What would you do if you were almost starving, out of work, and had no money. You ask the baker for some bread, but he refuses to give you any. Would you steal food to stay alive?

- A young man is in prison for theft. Who is guilty—the young person who stole something, his friends who led him on the wrong path, the people who raised him, or the person who saw him stealing and did nothing to stop him?

- In the West, originality is a hot item. Originality, however, is often based on an elaboration on other people's ideas. If you use other people's ideas, at what point is it stealing and when is it simply building on the ideas?

4. Self-Control

The *fourth abstinence* is about greed and sensuality. This is an important type of abstinence, particularly for teenagers whose hormonal changes make their sexual desires very strong. It is very important to practice self-control and moderation throughout life, but it is particularly important during this phase of it. This applies to the enjoyment of sex, food, alcohol, and drugs. Through this abstinence, young people also can learn not to take more than they need. Without moderation, people become the victim of their own desires. Ask the following questions to start a discussion:

1. If you are passionate about something, can you do it or enjoy it endlessly?
2. What is the difference between passion and greed?
3. Is greed an impulse you can control?
4. If you are aware of your desires, passions, and greed, what role does this "awareness" play?

5. Nonpossessiveness

The *fifth abstinence* is about freeing oneself from greed. For many young people, possessions are very important, and they don't want to have fewer than their friends have. This usually means the latest cell phone, clothes, video game, or computer. Talk with young people about their actual personal needs in terms of clothes, food, and even personal attention. Have them think about the effect these possessions have on their lives. This abstinence is closely related to the fourth abstinence. If you really know and have experienced who you are, greed falls away naturally.

The Five Precepts

The second part of yoga philosophy is formed by the five precepts. The precepts come after the abstinences and are about five habits for healthy self-development. You develop yourself through practicing purity, contentment, self-discipline, self-directed learning, and devotion.

1. Purity

The *first precept* is about cleanliness. This means cleanliness of body, clothing, food, and surroundings and also of thoughts, words, and actions. Purity encourages a healthy life and a clear head that allows for positive thoughts.

2. Contentment

The *second precept* is about thankfulness. This means being content with what you have. This thinking does not diminish the need to strive for improvement but, rather, it encourages the idea that improvement comes from dedication to humanity, animals, plants, earth, air, and water. In assuming this attitude, you come to appreciate the small things in life. You are at peace with everyone and accept who you are; you develop yourself from that sense of happiness and acceptance. Make sure young people understand that the contented feeling comes from consciousness and self-knowledge and not from possessing something.

3. Self-Discipline

Self-discipline, the *third precept,* helps young people develop positive habits such as self-control. Practicing this precept encourages young people to do what they really want to do and to be who they really want to be. It protects them from being swept along by random thoughts and feelings. Through self-discipline they can make choices through which their lives will become more ordered and better organized. In doing so, they find their own ways of working on self-discipline, such as practicing yoga each day, meditating, eating healthily, taking better care of themselves, or abstaining from using drugs.

4. Self-Directed Learning

Self-directed learning is the *fourth precept*. It is concerned with the discovery of the real self. Experiencing yourself consciously in relation to yourself and others—through questions such as "Who am I?" and "What is my purpose?"—is particularly important for young people. By talking with them about subjects they can think about, the process of self-awareness can be set in motion. In addition, meditation, reading, and keeping a journal can be a great help in finding the answers to life questions.

5. Devotion

The *fifth precept* is the most important of all. It is about devotion to the spiritual life and no longer being driven by your wants and desires. You can make this subject easier for young people to talk about by speaking of having confidence in your own strength and believing that you are okay as you are.

Practical Tips for the Teacher

Preparing the Lesson

It is important to prepare the lesson properly. Before you begin, take some time to think about the structure of the lesson, what you are going to tell the class (rules, agreements, length of time for the exercises, and signal to stop), and make sure you have all the necessary materials. Offer your students clarity and structure. In a school setting, there are always ground rules about what is or is not allowed during class time. When giving yoga classes outside of the school setting, it is important that you also make certain agreements. The most important of these would be:

- Do not laugh at other people.
- Do what you are told.
- Listen to each other.
- Cooperate with each other.
- Respect each other's limitations.

Fit your lesson to suit the atmosphere and mood. This may mean that a lesson turns out very differently from what you had envisioned. In some situations you may need to cut out some exercises because there is a greater need for a group discussion. It could also be that you need to think up a couple of extra exercises in case the ones you planned to do are not suitable for the people in the class.

You may choose to participate in the exercises yourself. This will depend on the type of exercise, the group, and what you have in mind. By not joining in you will have a better overview of the class; by joining in you can more easily activate the participants. The essential requirements for teaching yoga to young people are to have an enthusiastic and positive attitude and to be able to put yourself in their place. For example, you may find yourself asking, "Why are they acting this way?" when a student does not want to join in a particular exercise. In such cases, it is better not to try to force students. Young people need to be themselves, even if that means they don't dare or want to do something.

This book offers a variety of ways to introduce young people to yoga. The suggestions given here are far from being the only way of working. Be creative! You can put a lesson together by choosing a number of exercises from the book and putting your own slant on them. You might want to start with exercises for exploring the body, stretches for warming up, and yoga postures to keep the body strong and supple. To this add a relaxation exercise to calm down and a visualization to get away from the pressures of the day. Wrap things up with an exercise to wake up the class again. By switching from one type of exercise to another, you will keep the lesson interesting and varied.

The exercises do not need a certain length of time or a particular type of space. You can practice yoga indoors or outside. At school, you can teach a yoga class in an empty classroom or in the gym. At home, teenage students can choose their own location, finding a spot where they can retreat in peace to do yoga.

It is best to do yoga with bare feet as this gives you the best grip. At school, however, it may be compulsory to wear shoes to avoid health problems such as athlete's foot. In that case, the students can use gym shoes or acrobatic slippers with antislip soles.

I have found that when doing floor exercises, it is more comfortable to use a soft surface. I use rubber mats as they are good for insulation and give a good grip.

Choose a place where there is plenty of space to move, little distraction, good ventilation, and warmth. During the relaxation and visualization exercises you may wish to set the heat a little higher or let the participants cover themselves with a sheet as they will cool off while lying still.

Most of the exercises in this book are illustrated with a drawing. If the drawings differ a little from the description, follow the written instructions. Before you begin the lesson, go over a few practical tips with the participants (see page 12).

Key to the Icons Used in the Exercises

To help you find exercises suitable for a particular situation, each one is coded with symbols, or icons, that tell you the following things about the activity at a glance:

- the size of the group needed
- if the task is advanced
- if participants will exercise on a mat
- if a large space is required
- if musical accompaniment is required
- if physical contact is or might be involved

These icons are explained in more detail below.

The size of the group needed. While some exercises require partners, you can play many of them with any sized group.

  = The participants play individually, so any size group can play

  = The participants play in pairs

If a game is advanced. A few activities in this book should only be done by people with yoga experience or who are being supervised by a yoga professional. The more challenging activities are marked with the following icon:

  = For advanced children

If an exercise mat is required. Participants do yoga postures on the floor during some of the exercises. In those activities, a mat, rug, towel, or blanket might be used for the participants' comfort and safety.

 = Players will exercise on mats

If a large space is required. Almost all yoga exercises may be practiced in a relatively small space. However, a large space is ideal for some of the exercises, especially if you have a group of three or more people. The activities that require a large amount of space if a group is involved are marked with the following icon:

 = Large space needed

If music is required. Only a few exercises in this book require music. In those cases, soft, suitable music is suggested.

 = Music required

If physical contact is or might be involved. Although a certain amount of body contact might be acceptable in certain environments, the following icon has been inserted at the top of any exercise that might involve anything from a small amount of contact to minor collisions. You can figure out in advance if the activity is suitable for your participants and/or environment.

 = Physical contact likely

Tips for Teens

- Wear loose, comfortable clothes that let you move easily.
- If doing yoga after meals, eat a light meal. Doing yoga on a full stomach can hamper your movement.

- Sit comfortably with your back straight but relaxed. Pay attention to what the teacher is saying.

- By closing your eyes in certain exercises you will be better able to feel the effects the exercise has on your body, find out where your limits are, and experience how your body reacts.

- When you start an exercise, be aware of all the thoughts that come to you, but do not be distracted by your thoughts. If you notice that you are thinking about something else, stop and put your attention on your breathing. By making a habit of being aware of your thoughts, you will notice that you gain more control over them. Realize that it is you who keep your negative thoughts alive by constantly turning them over and over in your mind or by pretending that they do not exist.

- Take the time to get to know your body by investigating the shape and characteristics of its various parts and examining their differences through touch. Further, to assess the effect of a particular exercise on your body, touch the various parts of your body before and after so that you can feel how your body has reacted.

- If you experience resistance to a particular exercise, explore that reaction. Find out where the resistance comes from and see if you can find a way to deal with it. By discovering what you enjoy and what you do not enjoy you develop insight into yourself. Yoga is concerned with self-awareness and the fact that you are the only person who can experience yourself.

- Observe discipline and regularity when you practice yoga and stay inquisitive. Do not let the exercises become a daily drudge; do each exercise as if you are doing it for the first time.

Research into the Experience of Teens Practicing Yoga

During her time studying pedagogy at University of Utrecht in the Netherlands, Sanna Maris researched the influence of yoga on the minds of young people. The results of this research are covered in this chapter. The process that follows was developed by talking with people in their teens and twenties.

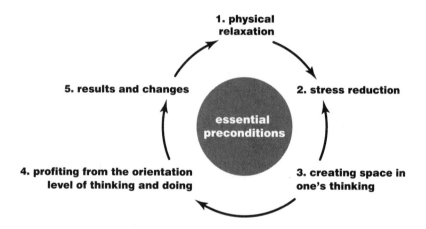

Physical Relaxation

Among other ways, physical relaxation is expressed through the power of the exercises, the amount of energy necessary for the exercises ("pretty heavy"), the feeling of tingling in the body, the efficiency of the exercises, the stretching and flexing of the muscles, and the experience of leaving the lesson filled with energy. Many young people admitted that they felt more mentally relaxed after the yoga class than before. Further, they said yoga had taught them how to relax physically.

"When I do the exercises, my body rests. While I'm doing an exercise and when I have finished, I feel completely peaceful and all my muscles are relaxed. The yoga exercises help to make or keep the muscles flexible."

– male student, 22 years old

The postures used during the classes seemed a bit strange at first:

"Then you think 'What on earth am I doing? What kinds of weirdoes are these?' you know…'Where are the hidden cameras?'"

– male student, 21 years old

"Well, at first, the first time you go, you think 'What the heck am I doing here?'"

– female student, 14 years old

While some of the young people continued coming to the classes because of the relaxation they experienced, another group mentioned a second physical result: a growth of physical awareness. These students agreed that they became more aware of pain and tension in their bodies. Breathing played an important role in the recognition of the limitations of their bodies. Through concentrating on their breathing they learned to let go of tension:

"I can bring my attention back to myself through my breathing and then I can find out where I am tense."

– male student, 22 years old

Stress Reduction

By practicing yoga, the students experienced a reduction in stress; yoga class became a point of rest in a busy week when they could let the weight fall from their shoulders. Many of them described their week as stressful, busy, or heavy; this is more or less normal in society today, and everyone recognizes these feelings. But during the yoga class they were able to let go of the pressure; yoga gave them the ability to come back to themselves. One of them described it as follows:

"It's as if you had an extra weekend in the middle of the week."

– female student, 18 years old

A number of people said that they fell asleep during the relaxation period—peace at last! Another way in which someone described the experience was of having an "empty head"—as if you have forgotten everything:

> "It is extremely relaxing; you forget everything for a while. For instance, you are sitting there and suddenly the light goes on and you had completely forgotten that you were in the gym, and ok, I just forgot that."
>
> *— male student, 16 years old*

Creating Space

In learning to relax, young people also gain more space in their heads. The more they relax, the easier it is to let go of problems and memories as they surface, creating more space in their minds. A number of students described their experiences, giving a clear picture of the effect yoga had on their problem-solving abilities:

> "I had all this stuff in my head, you know,…so much pressure, but by the end of the class it had all gone, right out of my head…I'd had a really hard week, you know, problems at home and stuff… but then I could really deal with it."
>
> *— male student, 16 years old*

> "Sometimes I really have to laugh, but that's more to do with certain postures setting off thoughts in my mind, or sometimes all these crazy thoughts come up…then I just have to laugh, and I suddenly think of all these jokes, but of course I can't tell them… sometimes old memories come up. It's not always nice or fun, but it definitely brings up a lot of stuff."
>
> *— male student, 22 years old*

Thinking and Doing

By creating some mental space, young people can find new solutions to their problems or new perspectives about the various levels of their development. In some students, this also results in a change in the way they do things (see Step 5 in the illustration on page 14). The group leader and the group itself also play a role in this growth process. The young people are encouraged to orientate themselves through the opinions and experiences of other young people. The resonance of someone else's words may help them confirm their own feelings; at the same time, different opinions and experiences help them to see new perspectives:

"I hear the conclusion, '[O]h, yes, that's interesting. I had never thought about it that way.'"

— male student, 17 years old

Some young students find this helps them reassess their own values, and that leads to a change in their behavior.

"They see it in a certain way, and then I look at how I see it and sometimes I think, '[N]o, that's not what I want.' But sometimes it's happened that I think—'[O]h, I could learn something from that, that says something to me, maybe I could use that in my own way, not their way, but just in my own way.'"

— male student, 16 years old

The teacher plays an important role in this orientation process between thought and action. By using particular themes, reading a story, or starting a discussion on a certain subject, the teacher can give the class something to think about—a new perspective. The students can use this perspective to find a new way of looking at their thought processes and their actions. Questions from the class may sometimes provide the impetus for orientational discussions or stories. This can be the first stimulus for students to get some perspective on their own thoughts and actions.

"You often act from impulsive thoughts that just pop up. If you learn to understand that, why you do things sometimes, you learn to know yourself. In turn, you can learn to take distance from it and then you don't do things out of impulse anymore."

— male student, 21 years old

The increased focus on the areas of thoughts and actions is stimulated from a more-intense experience of a thing as well as through the group and the teacher:

"It's not that you say things from not giving a f***, or something, you just say things, experience them more intensely than usual, which helps you to say this is absolutely not important, and that *is* important… it's sort of that the plus and minus of things, the positive and negative, just get bigger, there is a clearer difference between them. So some things get a lot more important and other things just fall away…."

– male student, 19 years old

Results and Changes

The young people agreed that practicing yoga helped them clear their heads. Yoga taught them to look at situations more coolly and then make conscious decisions instead of simply following their first impulse. It helped them create the space to look at their problems in another way and, in doing so, to act differently.

"Then I don't have to fly into a panic. I have learned that I can just think about things quietly."

– male student, 22 years old

Several of them spoke about finding more peace and quiet in their minds, so that they "first thought and then acted":

"You learn not to get aggressive so quickly. If something happens, you think about it, but more calmly. Then you know how to solve it, and you think more about how to do it right. For instance, let's take this one step at a time."

– female student, 15 years old

Another result is the development of self-awareness through concentrating on yourself. By concentrating on the physical exercises and in meditation on your thoughts, you are in a better state to concentrate on yourself:

"Yes, it's as if I'm sitting by myself in another room, and I don't hear anything around me and, yes, I feel more quiet."

– male student, 16 years old

Concentration also plays a significant part in the development of self-awareness:

> "If I've really got something on my mind, then I can think about it here really well–what I should do–and I don't really have a quiet place where I can think about what I should do…I had one really big problem, I'm not going to say what it was, but through yoga I took the right steps."
>
> *— male student, 21 years old*

> "Yoga really helps you to find quiet. You can see the whole picture, you could say. …all the stuff that's happened to me, things that were my fault if I had arguments and stuff. Or how you can solve problems."
>
> *— male student, 16 years old*

Essential Preconditions

The participants' attitudes toward yoga is the single greatest factor affecting how yoga is received by the group. Individual moods, as well as that of the group, also influence the experience. This was evident both physically and mentally.

> "After that operation I discovered that I had lived in a haze. Because my nose had been blocked the whole time, I couldn't hear or taste properly.… Now [that] I can breathe freely, the class has much more effect on me than it did before."
>
> *— male student, 23 years old*

We also noticed what influence fasting during Ramadan could have on the practice of yoga:

> "If I had eaten, then my body quickly became very warm, because your body starts working and the digestion too, so at that moment you feel the energy streaming through your body, because your body gets really warm and then I did yoga, and I notice that when I do yoga my body also gets really warm quickly, so that was sort of double…"
>
> *— female student, 16 years old*

The students felt that practicing yoga in a group increased their concentration. This was especially true if the group was quiet. Several students said how much they enjoyed having quiet lessons:

"I like doing yoga with quiet people, otherwise it doesn't have any point. Then you get wound up yourself because you automatically notice what the others are doing. I'm someone who has quite a bit of difficulty in concentrating if I have a lot of noise around me. So I prefer it when it's quiet to when it's noisy."

— female student, 14 years old

The teacher and the frequency of the classes also have an influence on participants' experiences.

Research Conclusions

Bringing about Awareness

The intent of this research was to study yoga's influence on young people in the 14- to 22-year-old age group. The results showed that the practice of yoga (for a minimum of ten lessons) can bring positive changes in the minds of young people. The physical and mental relaxation gave the young people space in their thinking—a point from which they were able to consider new possibilities for thinking and acting. Through the quietness and clarity of yoga and the support of the teacher and the other young people, the insight into their own thoughts and actions increased. Young people learned to reduce distractions by concentrating on themselves. Yoga allowed them to discover their inner experiences and create space in difficult situations so that with a relaxed mind they could choose how to react. In a situation where they might ordinarily react angrily, they were able to respond in a positive way by being quiet for a moment and ordering their thoughts. In this sense, yoga is an important technique for bringing about an awareness that, in turn, leads to positive behavior.

Support in the Development Process

Opinions on the use of yoga for therapeutic purposes are divided. Yoga clearly supports students whether or not they have problems, but some students indicated that yoga had a positive influence on their minds as well. If yoga supports the development process in young people, it may well be helpful in changing the behavior of students who have a problematic development process.

In thinking about this, it is important to consider the personal commitment that the practice of yoga requires. The use of yoga in psychiatry, for example, could be risky. All kinds of tensions, memories, and problems could be released, and it could be debated whether a person with a depressive or psychotic background would be able to process this information. You do not want a young student to swim alone in a river of memories, tensions, and problems, so if you want to use yoga in such a situation, you would want to engage a therapeutic guide as well. One strength in practicing yoga is that after a while, the young person will have learned a complete system that he can use to stay healthy. The use of yoga as a support for the personal development of the young person can therefore be recommended, but potential problems should be kept in mind to avoid any negative experiences for a new participant.

Interrupting the Stream of Thought
Practicing yoga ensures that—even for just a few moments—a young person can escape the day's endless stream of thoughts and find space to reflect on their actions. People think all day long, and they are being influenced by their thoughts. Thinking positive thoughts, for instance, helps a person stay positive; focusing on problems can bring depression; and thinking angry thoughts can leave a person feeling angry or negative.

Yoga ensures that this wild river of thought—the one in which young people have to paddle for all they are worth to avoid drowning—becomes a calm, babbling brook. Its practice gives a young person time to sit calmly in her boat, trailing her legs in the water, and gazing into the depths of the river. Through yoga, students free up their attention, which is usually focused on their thoughts, and learn to pay attention to their breathing, their movements, and the position of their bodies.

When young people learn to concentrate, they find peace in their thinking even outside the yoga class. The skill lies in learning to ignore your thoughts. By concentrating on your breathing, consciousness, and body parts, you finally find peace of mind. And somehow, over the course of the yoga lesson, the river of thoughts slows to a smooth, steady flow. By quietly observing your thoughts for what they are instead of instantly acting on them, you slowly come to know your spirit. Although you do nothing, you can see how you would normally have acted if you had had those thoughts. During meditation you let it all drift by you as "another of those waves of thought of which hundreds or thousands can come by in the day."

Exercises
and
Postures

Breathing Exercises

When young people observe their breathing patterns, they gain an idea of how they are feeling. They learn to be aware of whether they are breathing superficially, deeply, quickly, or slowly, and they begin to notice which part of the body is being oxygenated. Cramped breathing indicates emotional upset–the basis of stress. Gentle, regular breathing indicates a state of balance. Although emotions influence breathing and it is difficult to master your emotions, breathing can be mastered.

Such scrutiny also reveals there is a relationship between the nostrils, the breath, and the hemispheres of the brain, with changes taking place throughout the day. One nostril dominates at one moment, and the other nostril controls another moment. The right nostril represents the energy you are projecting, and the left nostril is the energy you are receiving. Harmony depends on the balance between these two types of energy. When you wake up in the morning, try to feel which nostril is dominant. If you then step out of bed and put the corresponding foot on the floor first, you will be putting your best foot forward.

1 Balancing the Breath

- Sit in a comfortable position.
- Hold one hand under your nose and observe your breathing.
- Which nostril is the air coming from?
- Close your right nostril with the right thumb.
- Breathe in through your left nostril for a count of four.
- Close your left nostril with the left index finger; hold your breath for a count of four.

- Release your thumb and exhale through your right nostril for a count of eight.
- Now switch nostrils. Keep your left nostril closed and breathe in through the right nostril, then out through the left while closing the right nostril with your thumb.
- Repeat the sequence a few times.

2 Feeling the Breath

- Lie on your back with your arms by your sides.
- Draw up your knees, placing your feet flat on the floor.
- Place your hands loosely on your throat.
- Breathe gently and feel the air streaming in and out.
- Feel your breath going up and down.
- Place your hands on your stomach.
- Breathe in from the lower abdomen.
- Feel how your stomach rises and falls.
- Put your right hand in front of your mouth.
- Blow softly on your hand.
- Now blow harder.
- What do you notice?

3 Breath Scan

- Lie flat on the floor and close your eyes.
- Become conscious of each inhalation and exhalation without influencing the breath.
- See how the breath slowly enters the nose, fills the lungs, and streams out again.

- As you breathe in, visualize the oxygen filling your lungs and flowing to your left leg, knee, and foot.

- As you exhale, the air flows out of your left foot, back via your lungs to your nose and out again.

- Can you now feel a difference between your right and left legs?

- Any time you catch yourself thinking of anything other than your breathing or feeling anything other than your breathing, make a mental note of it and concentrate just on the breathing.

- Inhale and now let the breath go down to your right foot.

- Exhale and feel the breath move out from your right foot back to the lungs, the nose, and out again.

- Continue sending the oxygen around your body in this way.

- Send the oxygen to both hands, lower arms, elbows, upper arms, shoulders, chest, midriff, stomach, genitals, backside, lower back, upper back, neck, and head.

- Become aware of the sensation of sending your breath around the body like this. Feel the tingling in your body, feel your muscles becoming more and more relaxed, and notice which parts of the body are less relaxed.

- Continue to send oxygen to any parts that do not yet feel relaxed.

- Breathe in and, as you exhale, send the tension out of that part of your body on your breath.

- Continue with this as long as you want and, if necessary, give the same attention to any other parts of your body that need some extra pampering.

- Pay attention to the rest of your body.

- Move your fingers and toes a little, open your eyes, and slowly sit up.

4 Hearing the Breath

- Sit comfortably.
- Breathe gently and feel the air stream through you.
- Breathe in and, as you exhale, make the sound "OOOOOOOO."
- Where in your body do you feel the vibration of the sound?
- Now make the following sounds in turn: "FFFFFF," "SSSSSS," "AAAAA."
- What differences do you notice with the different sounds?

5 Counting Breaths

- Lie on your back and close your eyes.
- Become aware of the pattern of your breathing without influencing it.
- Become aware of how the air gently enters your nose, fills your lungs, and leaves the body again.
- Notice whether you are breathing with your stomach, your midriff, or the top part of the chest.
- Start by counting as you breathe, "Inhale, one; exhale, two; inhale, three; exhale, four; inhale, five; exhale, six...."
- If you think about anything other than your breathing or feel anything other than your breathing, concentrate again on your breathing: "Inhale, one; exhale, two; inhale, three...."
- Observe the characteristics of your breathing: the depth, the speed, if your breathing becomes slower and more relaxed, whether you breathe from the stomach or from the chest, whether the way you breathe helps to relax your body, etc.
- Pay attention to the rest of your body again.
- Move your fingers and toes a little, open your eyes, and slowly sit up.

Getting to Know the Body

The exercises in this part of the book can help young people who need more balance in their lives. The practice of simple, uncomplicated movement is aimed at helping them get to know their bodies. As students move, their attention is concentrated on the various parts of the body. They become aware of what moves and what does not. In this way, movements become conscious (i.e., they are no longer made just out of habit), and young people feel free to try out variations. After some practice the movements also become easier and less strenuous.

Yoga gives students the opportunity to work with both body and spirit —an experience they will take with them when they perform repetitive daily tasks. This experience is the student's first step toward becoming more aware of their body; it is one step toward the ultimate goal: the prevention of stress.

Head and Neck

6 Head

- Sit up straight in the position you find most comfortable.
- Concentrate your attention on your head.
- As you breathe in, slowly bend your head backward and let your mouth fall open.

- As you breathe out, slowly bend your head forward and make your mouth small.
- Repeat the exercise a few times in rhythm with your breathing.
- Bring your head back to its normal position and see how it feels.
- What did you experience?

7 Ears

- Sit up straight in the position you find most comfortable.
- Concentrate your attention on your ears.
- Touch your ears and feel the shape.
- Hold your ears between your thumb and forefinger.
- Follow the shape of the earlobe and outer edge (pinna/auricle) of the ear.
- Massage your ears by gently rolling your fingers.
- Pull your earlobes and scratch behind the ears.
- Stop touching them and become aware of how it feels.
- Listen to the sounds inside and around you.
- Consciously listen to the sounds to your left and right.
- What do you notice?

8 Eyes

- Sit up straight in the position you find most comfortable.
- Concentrate your attention on your eyes.
- With eyes closed, gently touch your eyes with your fingers to feel the shape of them.

- Massage your eyebrows by gently pinching them, starting at the inside and working outward.
- Stop the exercise and focus on how it feels now.
- Move your eyes as far as you can to the right while keeping your head still.
- Imagine that you can see all the way down your right side (shoulders, side, hip, leg and foot) and back up again.
- Move your eyes until they are looking straight ahead again.
- Rest your eyes and feel the difference between your right and left eyes.
- Repeat the exercise, this time moving your eyes to the left.

9 Mouth

- Sit up straight in the position you find most comfortable.
- Focus your attention on your mouth.
- Touch your mouth and feel the shape of it.
- Gently massage around your mouth.
- Stop the exercise and focus on how your mouth feels now.
- Breathe in and pull the left side of your mouth as far as you can to the left.
- Breathe out and relax the left side of your mouth.
- Repeat a couple of times.
- Stop and focus on how your mouth feels now.
- Repeat the exercise a couple of times on the right side.
- Stop and feel the difference between left and right.
- Make the facial expressions for the following emotions: happiness, anger, sadness, disappointment, pain, and pride.
- What do you experience when you make those expressions?

10 Nose

- Sit up straight in the position you find most comfortable.
- Concentrate your attention on your nose.
- Touch your nose with your hands and feel its shape.
- Breathe in and open up the left side of your nose as much as you can.
- Breathe out and relax the nose.
- Repeat a couple of times.
- Stop and focus on the difference between the right and left sides.
- Repeat the exercise a couple of times with the right side of the nose.

11 Neck

- Sit up straight in the position you find most comfortable.
- Focus your attention on your neck.
- Place your fingertips on the back of your head.
- Massage your head by stroking your fingers down and up again.
- Continue this for a few minutes.
- Stop and become aware of how it feels.

Back and Shoulders

12 Back

- Begin in the Diamond pose (Exercise #52).
- Bend forward until your forehead touches or almost touches the ground.
- Place your hands on your back.
- Focus your attention on your back.
- Make fists and drum softly on your lower back.
- Stop and pay attention to how your back feels now.

13 Shoulders

- Sit up straight in the position you find most comfortable.
- Focus your attention on your shoulders.
- Touch your shoulders with your hands, feeling the shape of them.
- Massage one shoulder, strongly kneading the muscles as you move from the neck toward the arm.
- Stop and be aware of how your shoulder feels now.
- Repeat the exercise with the other shoulder.
- Stop and feel the difference between your right and left sides.
- Breathe in and pull your shoulder blades backward.
- Breathe out and relax the shoulders.
- Stop and see how your shoulders feel now.

Arms, Hands, and Fingers

· · · · · · · · · · · ·

14 Arms

- Sit up straight in the position you find most comfortable.
- Focus your attention on your arms.
- Touch your left arm with your right hand, feeling the shape of it.
- Massage your arm from the armpit downward toward the hand and back.
- Massage the upper arm.
- Stop and feel the difference between right and left sides.
- Repeat the exercise on the other arm.

15 Wrists

- Sit up straight in the position you find most comfortable.
- Bring your hands up, level with your heart.
- Rotate your wrists outward a few times and then inward.
- Shake your hands loosely.
- Stop and focus on how your wrists feel now.

16 Hands

- Sit up straight in the position you find most comfortable.
- Focus your attention on your hands.
- Touch your left hand with your right hand and explore its shape.
- Massage your hand, stretching and twisting your fingers.
- Bend your fingers inward and outward.
- Stop and feel the difference between your right and left hands.
- Change hands and repeat the exercise.
- Stop and feel the difference now.
- Rub your hands together briskly so they get nice and warm.
- Stop and focus on how they feel now.
- What do you notice?

17 Thumb

- Sit up straight in the position you find most comfortable and close your eyes.
- Stick your thumbs in the air, making a tight fist with the fingers.
- Think about how you feel when everything is going well.
- Smile and say to yourself, "I value myself."
- Affirm this with a bold thumbs-up gesture.
- Take the time to let these thoughts and feelings of self-appreciation sink in. Then open your eyes.

18 Index Finger

- Sit up straight in the position you find most comfortable and close your eyes.

- Point your index finger and fold the others inward.

- Envision accepting another person just as they are.

- Smile and say to yourself, "Today I will try to point less at other people" and "I am responsible for my own feelings toward others."

- Take the time to let these thoughts and the feeling of responsibility sink in. Then open your eyes.

19 Middle Finger

- Sit up straight in the position you find most comfortable and close your eyes.

- Make a circle with your thumb and middle finger on both hands.

- Feel how the fingers make contact with each other.

- Your middle finger is the one that reminds you that in any situation you have the choice of whether to say "Yes" or "No."

- Smile and say to yourself, "Today I choose to make my own choice whenever the opportunity arises" and "I choose whether or not I will listen to the opinion of another person, and I will decide for myself what my choice will be."

- Take the time to let these thoughts and the feeling of freedom of choice sink in. Then open your eyes.

20 Ring Finger

- Sit up straight in the position you find most comfortable and close your eyes.
- Form a circle with the thumb and ring finger of each hand.
- Focus your attention on the ring finger and feel how this finger–which symbolizes commitment–feels when touched by the thumb.
- Think about what the word commitment means to you and how you deal with it.
- Think about what you really want to commit yourself to.
- Think how important it is to choose goals that are attainable so that you are not constantly disappointed.
- Smile and say to yourself, "Today I commit myself to the agreements I make with myself."
- Take the time to let these thoughts and the feeling of commitment sink in. Then open your eyes.

21 Little Finger

- Sit up straight in the position you find most comfortable and close your eyes.
- Form a circle with the thumb and little finger of each hand.
- Focus your attention on your little finger and take the time to consider what little means to you.
- Think of some small thing that has given you pleasure today.
- Smile and say to yourself, "Today I am open to enjoying the little things in life."
- Take the time to let these thoughts and the ability to take pleasure in small things sink in.

Chest and Stomach

22 Chest

- Sit up straight in the position you find most comfortable.
- Focus your attention on your chest.
- Touch your chest with your hands and feel how it fills with air as you breathe.
- Raise your arms and stretch them above your head.
- Feel the space that this creates between your ribs.
- Lower your arms again.
- Repeat the sequence several times.

23 Stomach

- Sit up straight in the position you find most comfortable.
- Focus your attention on your stomach.
- Think about your stomach.
- What do you experience?
- Touch your stomach with your hands and feel its size and shape.
- Inhale and pull your stomach in.
- Exhale and relax your stomach.
- Repeat the sequence several times.
- Place your hands on your stomach and wobble it gently.
- Stop and see how it feels now.

Hips (Pelvis) and Buttocks

24 Hips (Pelvis)

- Sit up straight in the position you find most comfortable.
- Focus your attention on your hips/pelvis.
- Touch the pelvic area with your hands and feel the shape.
- Feel whether both *ischia*, "sitting bones," are carrying equal weight.
- Feel the contact of your body with the floor.
- Roll back and forth by tipping your hips backward and forward.
- Keep the upper part of your body as still as you can.
- Let your hips move in rhythm with your breathing.
- Repeat the exercise several times, continuing in rhythm with your breathing.
- Stop and see how it feels now.

25 Buttocks

Students may find this game a little embarrassing and might laugh or make off-color comments; find a way to introduce the exercise in your own language to help them to get comfortable with it. You may even choose to substitute terms that they understand more easily.

- Start from the Mountain pose (Exercise #41).
- Concentrate your attention on your buttocks.

- Touch your buttocks with your hands and feel the shape.
- Tense your anal sphincter; then relax it.
- Breathe in and tense your buttocks.
- Breathe out and relax them again.
- Repeat the sequence several times.
- Your anal sphincter is related to the muscles around the mouth.
- Become aware of the feeling of tensing and relaxing the sphincter.
- What do you notice?

Legs and Feet

26 Legs

- Sit up straight in the position you find most comfortable.
- Concentrate your attention on your legs.
- Take your left leg in both hands.
- Massage the leg from the top downward and back again.
- Massage the upper part of your leg.
- Stop and feel the difference between your left and right legs.
- Repeat on the other leg.

27 Knees

- Sit up straight in the position you find most comfortable.
- Focus your attention on your knees.
- As you inhale, raise your knees. As you exhale, let them sink back down.
- Repeat several times in rhythm with your breathing.
- Stop and see how your knees feel now.

28 Ankles

- Sit up straight with your legs stretched out in front of you.
- Lift up your right thigh and hold it with both hands.
- Rotate your foot several times outward and then rotate it inward.
- Stop and feel the difference between your left and right ankles.
- Repeat the exercise with the left leg and foot.

29 Feet

While sitting:

- Sit up straight in the position you find most comfortable.
- Focus your attention on your feet.
- Take your left foot in your hands.
- Massage the top and underside of the foot, pull on your toes, twist them from left to right, make a fist with your hand and drum lightly on the sole.
- Grasp the ankle and shake the foot until it feels loose.
- Stop and feel the difference between your left and right foot.
- Repeat with the other foot.

While standing:

- Stand upright in the Mountain pose (Exercise #41).
- Focus your attention on your feet and feel how they make contact with the floor.
- Rock back and forth a few times from toes to heels and from the insides to the outsides of your feet.
- Stop and focus on how your feet feel now.

Stretching
Exercises

As preparation for the yoga postures you can begin by doing a few simple stretching (stretch and flex) exercises to loosen the body. The stretching exercises can also be used for cooling down, after exercising, to calm the body down again. During the stretching exercises, ask the students to focus their attention on the muscles that are stretched. When the muscles are fully stretched, they will feel some slight tension. This tension will decrease as they hold the posture.

During these exercises, remind the students to keep up a gentle breathing rhythm. They should not hold their breaths. Have them hold each pose for a few seconds so that they can really feel what each exercise does to the body. Encourage them to use their breathing as much as possible to keep the body relaxed during these stretching exercises.

30 Calf Stretch

- Find a space where you can lean against the wall.
- Stand a short distance from the wall.
- Place your right hand on your left hand and push against the wall with arms bent.
- Lean your head on your arms.
- Bend the front knee and push it against the wall.
- Stretch the other leg, keeping your foot flat on the floor.
- Bend your hips forward while still keeping the back leg stretched.
- Stop and feel the difference between your left and right calves.
- Repeat the exercise with the other leg.

31 Leg Stretch

- Lie down on your back.
- Pull your right knee up to your chest and clasp it with your hands.
- Make sure that your head and lower back remain on the floor.
- Pull your leg firmly to your chest.
- Relax and feel the difference between the two legs.
- Repeat on the left leg.

32 Crotch Stretch

- Start by sitting cross-legged (Tailor pose; Exercise #51).
- Place the soles of your feet together and take your feet in your hands.
- Bend forward from the hips, keeping your back straight.
- Push your knees gently to the floor.
- Hold the position for a moment and then return to the original position.

33 Arm Stretch

- Start in the Tailor pose (Exercise #51).
- Place your right hand at the top of your back.
- Put your left hand on your right elbow.
- Breathe in and stretch your right hand backward.
- Breathe out and relax your right hand.
- Repeat this several times in rhythm with your breathing.

- Stop and become aware of the difference between your right and left arms.
- Repeat the exercise with the other arm.

34 Hand Stretch

- Sit up straight in the position you find most comfortable.
- Fold your hands in front of you with fingertips pointing upward.
- Push your palms and fingertips together.
- Remain in this position, breathing gently and evenly.
- Stop the exercise and focus on how you feel.

35 Finger Stretch

- Hold your right hand in front of you at chest height with the palm toward you.
- Take your right little finger in your left hand.
- Inhaling, bend your little finger backward. Exhaling, let it come back to its natural position.
- Do this with each finger in turn.
- Now repeat with the fingers of the left hand.

36 Back Stretch

- Sit up straight and pull your knees toward your chest.
- Gently roll over backward with your chin tucked into your chest.
- Roll backward and forward until you feel that your back is more flexible.

37 Diagonal Stretch

- Lie on your back with eyes closed.
- Breathe in, bringing your left hand up. Put your left hand on the floor behind your head.
- Stretch the left side of your body as far as you can, holding your breath for a moment.
- As you breathe out, bring your hand back to your side.
- Relax your left side and be aware of how it feels now.
- What differences can you feel between the right and left sides of your body?
- Repeat the exercise with the right side of your body.
- Open your eyes and sit up slowly.

38 Twist Stretch

- Lie on your back with eyes closed.
- Stretch your arms out sideways at shoulder level with palms upward.
- Pull your legs up toward your chest, keeping your soles flat on the floor.
- Breathe in. As you breathe out, let your knees fall gently to the left and turn your head to the right.
- Breathe in, and bring your legs back up again while turning your head back to the middle.
- As you breathe out, let your legs fall gently to the right and turn your head to the left.
- Repeat the exercise several times in rhythm with your breathing.
- Open your eyes and sit up slowly.

39 Moon Stretch

- Lie on your back with eyes closed.
- Raise your head, turn it to the left, and then let it down to the ground again.
- Move the left leg to the left and slide the right leg up against it.
- Let your trunk lie still and breathe to the left.
- Remain in this position with your eyes closed for a moment or two.
- Return to the first position.
- What differences can you feel between the right and left sides of your body?
- Repeat the exercise on the other side of the body.
- Open your eyes and sit up slowly.

40 Frogman Stretch

- Lie on your back with eyes closed.
- Pull your knees up and place the soles of your feet together.
- Let your knees drop outward.
- Bring your arms up above your head.
- Bend your elbows so your fingertips touch.
- Feel how your back makes contact with the floor.
- Each time you breathe out, relax your thighs.
- Lie still for a moment with eyes closed.
- Open your eyes and sit up slowly.

Movement Exercises

In each of these postures the spinal column bends or stretches, to ensure that the body stays supple. These postures have a positive influence on mind and body. No prior experience is necessary for the postures in this chapter.

The exercises are divided into static and dynamic positions. The dynamic postures consist of a series of linked positions that are performed one after the other when you inhale and exhale. You can do these sequences several times over, as long as you enjoy it. The static postures are done at a slower tempo, are held for a longer time, and have a stronger effect. The static postures are divided into standing postures that give power and balance, sitting postures that are relaxing, reversed postures that give energy, reversed postures that are cleansing, and supine postures that are relaxing.

In some of the exercises, teens learn to work together and to sense and respect each other's limitations.

Standing Poses

Standing postures give balance and equilibrium and a grounding with the earth. The initial position for all of these postures is the Mountain pose.

41 Mountain

- Stand up straight with your arms by your sides.
- Place your feet slightly apart, in line with your shoulders.
- Bend the knees very slightly to avoid having them locked.
- Focus your attention on your feet. Feel the pressure of the ground on the different parts of each foot.
- Divide your weight evenly between the two feet.
- Relax your buttocks, shoulders, and arms.
- Keep your head straight by imagining a cord fastened to the crown of your head that is gently pulled upward.

42 Tree

- Stand up straight in the Mountain pose (Exercise #41).
- Move your weight to your right foot.
- Bend your right knee slightly and grasp your left ankle in your right hand.
- Place the left foot against the inside of your right knee and stretch the right leg.
- Fold your hands in front of your chest and raise them in the air.
- Hold this position as long as you remain balanced.
- Return to the Mountain pose.
- Repeat the exercise standing on the other leg.

43 Dancer 1

- Stand up straight in the Mountain pose (Exercise #41).
- Place your weight on your left foot.
- Bend your right leg backward and take your foot in your right hand.
- Pull that foot as close as you can toward your buttocks.
- Inhale and then stretch your left arm above your head.
- Pull your right foot as close to your buttock as you can and keep breathing.
- Remain in this position as long as you remain balanced.
- Return to the Mountain pose.
- Repeat the exercise on the other leg.

44 Dancer 2

- Begin from the fourth instruction in Dancer 1 (Exercise #43).
- Breathe in and stretch your left arm above your head.
- Breathe out and bend forward with your left arm pointing forward.
- Pull your right leg upward and breathe gently and evenly.
- Remain in this position as long as you remain balanced.
- Return to the Mountain pose (Exercise #41).
- Repeat the exercise on the other leg.

45 Warrior 1

- Stand up straight with legs apart.
- Point your right foot forward and your left foot to the side.
- Swivel your body in the direction of your left foot.
- Inhale. Bring your arms upward to the side and stretch them up over your head.
- Put your palms together.
- Exhale and bend your left knee forward.
- Hold this position as long as you can remain balanced.
- Return to the Mountain pose (Exercise #41).
- Repeat the exercise with the other leg.

46 Warrior 2

- Stand up straight with legs apart.
- Point the right foot forward and the left foot to the side.
- Breathe in and raise your arms sideways to shoulder height.
- Breathe out and bend the left knee forward.
- Look at the fingers of your left hand.
- Hold this position as long as you can remain balanced and breathe evenly.
- Return to the Mountain pose (Exercise #41).
- Repeat the exercise with the other leg.

47 Woodcutter

- Stand up straight with legs apart.
- Clasp your hands together.
- Breathe in and raise your arms until you stretch them above your head.
- As you breathe out, bend forward, bringing your arms down and through your legs, pointing behind you.
- Repeat the exercise several times in time with your breathing.

48 Eagle

- Stand up straight in the Mountain pose (Exercise #41).

- Bend your right arm and bring your hand up to eye level.

- Put your left hand through the crook of your right arm.

- Twist the arms around each other and put the palms together.

- Cross your right leg over your left leg and hook your toes around your calf.

- Keeping your arms and legs entwined, inhale while straightening your legs and stretching your arms upward.

- Hold this position as long as you can remain balanced.

- Return to the Mountain pose.

- Repeat the exercise with the opposite arm and leg.

49 Airplane

- Stand up straight in the Mountain pose (Exercise #41).
- Breathe in and raise your arms outward at shoulder level.
- Exhale and lean forward, putting your weight on your left leg and lifting your right leg out behind you.
- Remain in this position as long as you can remain balanced.
- Return to the Mountain pose.
- Repeat the exercise standing on the other leg.

50 Chair

- Stand up straight in the Mountain pose (Exercise #41).
- Inhale and stretch your arms out in front of you at shoulder level.
- Breathe out and bend your knees as if sitting down.
- Keep the upper part of your body straight.
- Hold this position as long as you can, breathing evenly.
- Return to the Mountain pose.
- Repeat the sequence several times.

Floor Exercises

For the floor exercises, students can sit in several different ways. Remind them of the following:

- Keep your back straight.
- Keep your head straight with your chin tucked in.
- Strive for as little tension as possible in your neck and shoulders.
- Relax your jaws and close your eyes.
- Remember these points each time you sit down.

Below are a number of suggestions for ways you can begin the exercise. Choose the one that your students find most comfortable.

51 Tailor

- Sit on the floor with your legs stretched out in front of you.
- Cross your legs and pull your ankles toward your body.
- Let the knees drop as close to the floor as possible.
- Place your hands on your knees.

52 Diamond

- Sit on your knees.
- Place the palms of your hands on your thighs.

53 Mouse

- Start from the Diamond pose (Exercise #52).
- Lean over until your forehead touches the ground.

- Lay your hands on the ground behind you, with your arms by your sides.
- Close your eyes and hold this position.
- Slowly sit up again.

54 Half Moon

- Start from the Diamond pose (Exercise #52).
- Stretch your thighs by sitting up with your weight on your knees, and then swing your left leg to the side.
- Keep your arms by your sides.
- Breathe in and raise your arms sideways to shoulder height.
- Breathe out and bend over to the left.
- Look up at the ceiling.
- Make sure not to lean forward and to keep your upper body and arms in the same plane as your outstretched leg.
- Breathe evenly and hold the position for as long as it is comfortable to do so.
- Breathe in and come back to a vertical position.
- Breathe out and drop your arms to your sides.
- Return to the Diamond pose and note the difference between your right and left sides.
- Repeat the exercise with your right leg stretched out.
- Repeat the exercise a few times on each side.

55 Camel

- Sit on your knees.
- Breathe in and raise your body.
- Breathe out and carefully bend over backward, placing your hands on your buttocks.
- Carefully put your hands flat on your feet and look upward.
- Breathe gently and hold this position for as long as it is comfortable.
- Return to the first position.
- Repeat the sequence twice.
- Rest in the Mouse pose (Exercise #53).
- After a moment, gently sit up.

56 Boat

- Sit down with your legs bent. Put your feet flat on the floor.
- Lift your feet from the floor and stretch your arms forward parallel with the ground. Carefully raise your legs, keeping them straight while your upper body reclines backward.

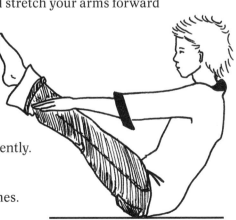

- Hold this position for as long as it is comfortable, breathing gently.
- Return to the original position.
- Repeat the sequence several times.

57 Cow

- Start on your hands and knees.
- Place your left foot on the ground in front of your right knee.
- Slide your left leg along the outside of your right leg and sit on your right heel. If you wish, you can slide your right foot out to the left so you sit on the ground.
- Inhale and raise both arms.
- Exhale. Place your right hand behind your head and your left hand on your lower back.
- Move your hands toward each other and try to shake hands with yourself.
- Hold the pose for as long as it is comfortable. Breathe gently.
- Go back to the starting position.
- Be aware of the differences between your left and right sides.
- Repeat the exercise, using the opposite legs and arms.

58 Turtle

- Sit on the floor with your legs spread apart.
- Inhale and raise your arms.
- Exhale and lean forward, bringing your head down to the floor.
- Put your arms under your knees and reach backward with palms upward.
- Breathe gently and hold this position for as long as it feels comfortable.

- Slowly sit upright again.
- Repeat the sequence several times.

59 Bow and Arrow

- Sit on the ground with your legs stretched out in front of you.
- Place your right foot against the inside of your left thigh.
- Grasp the big toe or arch of your right foot in your right hand.
- Place your left hand flat on the floor next to your hip.
- Inhale and raise your right leg as high as you can, keeping it straight.

- Exhale and lower your leg.
- Repeat the exercise.
- Return to the first position.
- Repeat the exercise, raising the left leg.

60 Cat 1

- Start on your hands and knees with your fingers spread on the ground.
- Breathe in and drop your stomach, raise your buttocks, and pull your head backward.
- Breathe out, raise your back, and drop your buttocks and head.
- Repeat the exercise several times in rhythm with your breathing.

61 Cat 2

- Start from the Cat 1 position as described above.
- Breathe in and stretch your left leg out behind you and your right arm out in front of you.

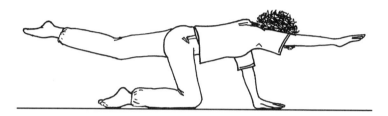

- Breathe out, bring your left leg forward, drop your head, and try to touch your knee to your nose (keep your right arm up if you can).
- Repeat several times in rhythm with your breathing.
- Repeat the exercise with the right leg.

62 Downward-Facing Dog

- Start on your hands and knees and spread your fingers on the ground.
- Breathe in and lift your body and buttocks in the air.
- Stretch your arms and legs.
- Put your feet flat on the floor.
- Look at your navel.

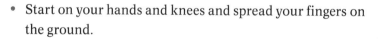

- Hold this position for as long as you can comfortably.
- Return to the starting position.
- Repeat the sequence several times.

63 Slide

- Sit on the floor with your legs straight out in front of you, toes pointing upward.
- Lean back a little and put your hands flat on the floor directly below your shoulders, fingers facing forward.
- Breathe in and lift your bottom, pushing up through your pelvis, straightening your legs, and pressing your feet toward the floor till your torso and legs are in a straight line and your body forms a flat inclined plane.

- Hold this position for as long as it is comfortable and be sure to breathe evenly.
- Return to the first position.
- Repeat the sequence several times.

64 Bow

- Start by lying on your stomach.
- Bend your legs at your knees so you can grasp your ankles with your hands.
- Breathe in, pulling your body up and keeping your arms stretched.
- Breathe out and come down again.
- Relax your arms by letting go of your ankles.

- Repeat the sequence several times.
- Rest in the Mouse pose (Exercise #53).

65 Wheel

- Start by lying on your back.
- Bend your legs and bring your feet flat on the floor as close as you can to your buttocks.
- Place your hands flat on the floor next to your head, palms down.
- Breathe in, stretching your arms and legs so that your body forms a bow.
- Hold this position for as long as it is comfortable; breathe evenly.
- Return to the lying position.
- Repeat the sequence several times.
- Finally, return to the lying position. Roll onto your stomach and come to rest in the Mouse pose (Exercise #53).

66 Bridge

- Start by lying on your back.
- Bend your legs and place your feet flat on the floor.
- Lay your arms by your sides with your palms down.
- Breathe in and raise your hips and chest until your thighs are just about parallel to the floor.
- Hold this position for as long as it is comfortable, breathing evenly.

- Lie on your back again.
- Repeat the sequence several times.

Note: If necessary for comfort, place a thickly folded blanket under the neck during this exercise.

67 Table

- Sit with your legs bent. Place your feet flat on the floor.
- Place your hands on the floor next to your hips with fingers pointing forward.
- Breathe in and raise your buttocks from the floor until your thighs and upper body are flat and parallel to the ground.
- Stretch your arms and bend your neck backward.

- Hold this position for as long as it is comfortable, breathing evenly.
- Return to the starting position.
- Repeat the sequence several times.

68 Fish

- Start by lying flat on your back.
- Bend your arms and come up on your elbows.
- Raise your neck, shoulders, and chest, arching your back and dropping the crown of your head back toward the floor.
- Close your eyes and breathe evenly.
- Hold this position as long as you can and breathe gently.
- Slowly return to the starting position.

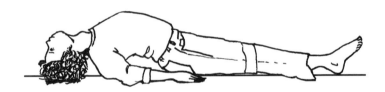

69 Sprinter

- Start from Downward-Facing Dog (Exercise #62) on hands and feet.
- Place your hands flat on the floor at shoulder level.
- Bring your left foot forward and place it between your hands.
- Stretch your right leg out backward.
- Hold this position and breathe evenly.

- Return to the starting position.
- Repeat the exercise starting with the opposite foot forward.

70 Dove

- Start from the Sprinter posture (Exercise #69), with your right foot between your hands.
- Let your right leg drop to the floor parallel with your hips.
- Stretch out your left leg so that the top of your foot is flat on the floor.
- Walk forward on your hands as far as you can and bring your head down to the ground.
- Hold this position for as long as it is comfortable, breathing evenly.

- Return to the starting position.
- Repeat the exercise starting with the opposite foot forward.
- Become aware of the differences between your right and left sides.

71 Cobra

- Start by lying on your stomach.
- Place your hands flat on the floor at chest level.
- Rest your forehead on the floor.
- Inhale and push yourself up by straightening your arms.
- Exhale and come back down.
- Repeat the exercise a few times.
- Rest in the Mouse pose (Exercise #53).

72 Cricket

- Start by lying on your stomach.
- Your arms are by your sides with palms on the floor.
- Inhale and raise your left leg.

- Exhale and lower your left leg.
- Repeat the sequence several times, changing legs.

73 Candle

- Start by lying on your back.
- Bring your knees up to your chest.
- Bend your arms and support your lower back with your hands.
- Breathe in and raise your legs in the air.
- Make your back as straight as you can and keep your shoulders on the ground.
- Breathe gently and evenly and hold the position for as long as it remains comfortable.
- Slowly return to the starting position.
- Repeat the sequence several times.

74 Plow

- Start from the Candle pose (Exercise #73).
- Gently lower your feet so they rest on the floor behind your head, keeping your legs stretched.
- Lay your hands on the ground for support.
- Hold this posture for as long as it feels comfortable.
- Unroll slowly, lie on your back, and rest for a moment.
- Repeat the sequence a few times.

Relaxation Poses

Silence and rest are important for the body, just as action and movement are. Yoga is a way of discovering the body through movement. Relaxing postures will help students discover the pleasure of silence after movement.

75 Back Position

- Lie on your back with your legs slightly apart and in line with your shoulders.
- Lay your arms by your sides, palms upward.
- Your fingers should point toward your toes.
- Tilt your head back so that your chin points upward.

76 Stomach Position

- Lie on your stomach with your arms by your sides.
- Turn your palms upward.
- Put your forehead on the ground.

77 Side Position

- Lie on your right side.
- Pull up your knees.
- Lay your head on your arms.

78 Legs Up

- Sit close to the wall with your right side facing it (in other words, your torso should be perpendicular to the wall).
- Breathe in, and while bringing your back, shoulders, and head slowly down to the floor, raise your closed and straightened legs upward against the wall until they are vertical.
- Lay your arms by your sides on the floor.
- Try to keep your buttocks as close as you can to the wall and to keep your legs straight.
- Breathe gently and hold this position for as long as you are comfortable.
- Open your eyes and sit up slowly.

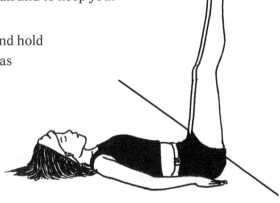

79 Tensing and Relaxing

- Start by lying on your back with eyes closed.
- As you breathe in, tense up different parts of your body one at a time.
- Begin with your head, neck, shoulders, arms, hands, stomach, buttocks, legs, and feet.
- As you breathe out, relax each part again.
- Finally tense your whole body at the same time as you inhale, then relax everything as you breathe out.
- Open your eyes again and slowly sit up.

80 Limb Lifting

- Start by lying on your back with your eyes closed.
- As you breathe in, lift different limbs in turn.
- Begin with your head, left arm, right arm, left leg, and right leg.
- As you breathe out, lower the limbs gently back down to the floor.
- Open your eyes and sit up slowly.

Dynamic Poses

81 Sun Dance

1. Stand up straight (Mountain pose; Exercise #41).

2. Breathe in, bring your hands outward and upward, and stretch them above your head. Imagine you are looking at the sun and feel the warmth on your body.

3. Breathe out and lower your hands, lean over forward, and place your hands on the ground next to your feet with fingers pointing forward.

4. Breathe in and step or jump backward with both feet. Push your buttocks up in the air and look at your navel (Downward-Facing Dog pose; Exercise #62).

5. Breathe out, drop your buttocks onto your heels, and stretch your arms forward as far as you can.

6. Breathe in, slide your upper body forward, and stretch your arms. Your upper body is not touching the floor (Cobra pose; Exercise #71).

7. Breathe out and push your buttocks up in the air again, stretch your legs and look at your navel (Downward-Facing Dog pose).

8. Step or jump forward so that your legs are between your hands.

To complete the sequence, breathe in and stand up slowly (Mountain pose). Repeat the sequence several times.

Sun Dance

82 Moon Dance

1. Stand up straight (Mountain pose; Exercise #41).

2. Breathe in and raise your arms outward and upward until they are above your head. Place your palms together with fingers pointing upward (called Stretch pose).

3. Breathe out and bring your hands down in front of your chest (called Prayer pose).

4. Breathe in and stretch your arms outward above your head, separating your palms. Imagine that you are looking at the moon and that you can feel the moon's power.

5. Breathe out, bend your knees outward, and squat as you bring your palms together in front of your chest (called Squatting pose).

6. Breathe in and turn toward the right. Bring your left knee to the floor and the right knee out sideways. Stretch your arms out to the sides and turn your neck as far as you can to the right, looking over your shoulder.

7. Breathe out, bring your head back to face forward, and bring your palms together in front of your chest (Squatting pose).

8. Breathe in, turning your body to the left. Bring your right knee down to the floor and turn your left knee outward. Stretch your arms out to the sides and turn your neck as far as you can to the left, looking over your shoulder.

9. Breathe out and return to the Squatting pose.

To complete the sequence, breathe in and slowly stand up (Mountain pose). Repeat the cycle several times.

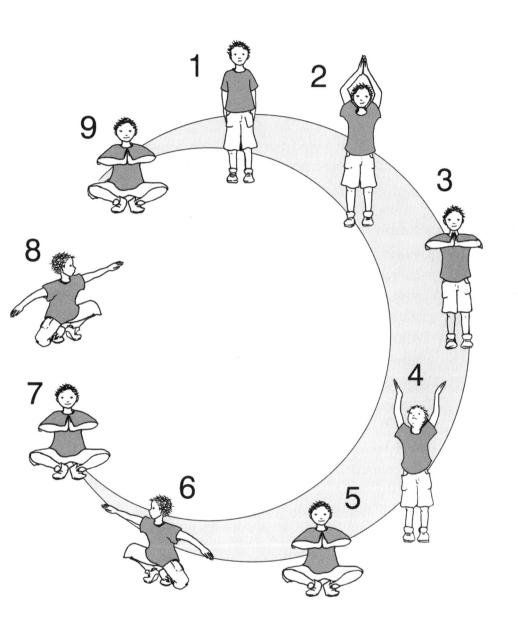

Moon Dance

83 Star Dance

1. Stand up straight (Mountain pose; Exercise #41).

2. Breathe in, lift your arms outward and upward, and stretch your hands above your head.

3. Breathe out and bend over forward, placing your hands on the ground (called Forward Bend).

4. Breathe in and step or jump backward. Push your buttocks up and look at your navel (Downward-Facing Dog pose; Exercise #62).

5. Breathe out and turn your left hip and left foot a quarter turn to the right. Place your right foot on the side of your left foot and stretch your right arm upward. Imagine that you are looking at the stars and catching one with your hand. Hold this position for a few moments, breathing evenly.

6. Place both hands and feet on the ground again and look at your navel (Downward-Facing Dog pose).

7. Turn your right hip and right foot a quarter turn to the left. Put your left foot on the side of your right foot and stretch your left arm. Hold this position and breathe gently.

8. Place both hands and feet on the ground again and look at your navel (Downward-Facing Dog pose).

9. Step or jump forward and place both hands on the floor.

To complete the sequence, slowly stand up again and stand straight with your arms by your sides (Mountain pose). Repeat the sequence.

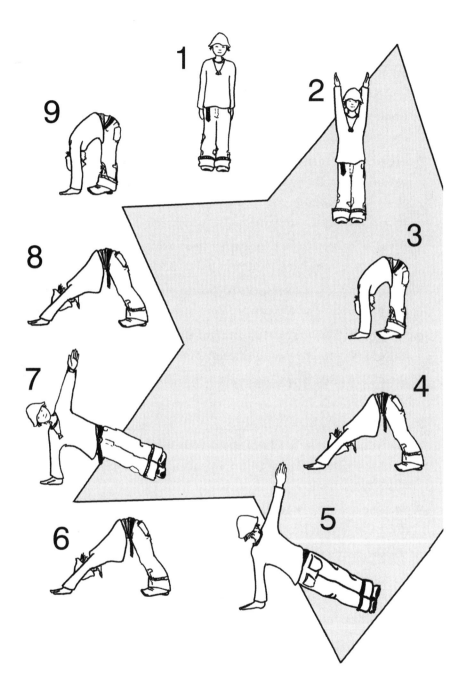

Star Dance

84 Earth Dance

1. Stand up straight with your hands together in front of your chest, fingers pointing upward (Prayer pose; see Exercise #82).

2. Breathe in, and with your palms still together, bring your hands up, stretching them above your head.

3. Breathe out. Turn your trunk to the right, letting your arms drop so that your right hand is a little above your head and your left is at waist level, hands open, palms facing forward. Look at the fingers of your right hand.

4. Breathe in, turn to face forward, raise your arms, and stretch them above your head with your palms back together.

5. Breathe out. Bend over forward, place your hands flat on the floor, and look behind you (Forward Bend pose; see Exercise #83).

6. Breathe in. Slowly stand up straight and put your hands together in front of your chest with fingers pointing upward (Prayer pose).

7. Breathe in and bring your arms up, stretching your hands above your head.

8. Breathe out. Turn your body to the left, letting your arms drop so that your left hand is a little above your head and your right is at waist level, hands open, palms facing forward. Look at the fingers of your left hand.

9. Breathe in and turn to face forward. Raise your arms and stretch them above your head (Stretch pose).

Repeat this sequence (1 through 9) several times.

10. To complete the exercise, breathe out. Bend over forward, place your hands flat on the floor, and look at the ground or behind you (Forward Bend).

Then breathe in, slowly stand up straight, and put your hands together in front of your chest with fingers pointing upward (Prayer pose).

Repeat the whole exercise several times.

1

2

3

4

5

6

7

8

9

10

Earth Dance

85 Sky Dance

1. Stand up straight with your hands behind you and your fingers laced together.

2. Breathe in and bring your arms up behind you as far as you can.

3. Breathe out and bend forward from the hips.

4. Hold your breath for a moment and let your hands hang down.

5. Breathe in and stand up slowly, uncurling your back as you do (Mountain pose; Exercise #41).

6. Stretch your hands out sideways and up above your head with palms facing upward.

7. Breathe out and bring your arms outward and down with your palms facing downward (Mountain pose).

Repeat the whole sequence a few times.

Sky Dance

Partner Poses

86 Rising Hands

- Squat facing your partner.
- Hold hands with your fingers entwined.
- Breathe in, stand up, and bring your arms out sideways and up above your heads.
- Breathe out, bring the arms down again, and sit on your heels again.
- Repeat the sequence several times.

87 Dancers

- Stand up, facing each other.
- Hold hands (one partner gives her right hand, and the other takes it with his left).
- Place your weight on the foot on the same side as the hand you are holding with your partner and take your other foot in your other hand (see illustration).
- Breathe in and raise the arm that is holding your foot.
- Breathe out and carefully bend forward.
- Breathe gently and hold this pose, keeping each other in balance.

- Return to the starting position.
- Repeat the exercise, changing legs.

88 Candles

- Lie on your backs, head to head with the tops of your heads just touching.
- Spread your arms out sideways and up slightly to take each other's hands.
- Lift your legs in the air.
- Try to raise yourself up so that your toes touch.
- Breathe gently and hold this position, keeping each other in balance.
- Return to the first position.
- Repeat the sequence a few times.

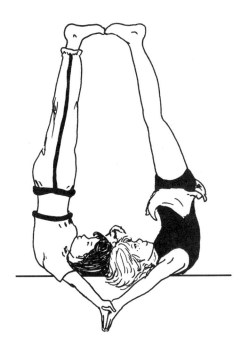

---

89 Camels

- Sit on your heels, back to back with your partner.
- Stretch your arms above your heads and take hold of each other's hands.
- Breathe in, lift your buttocks from your heels, and carefully lean back.
- Keep each other in balance and hold the pose.
- Let go of each other's hands and lean forward until your head touches the ground.
- Breathing gently, hold this position.
- Return to the first position.
- Repeat the sequence several times.

90 Leg Pushing

- Start on your hands and knees.
- Your buttocks are facing each other but are not touching.
- One of you lifts your right leg, and the other lifts the left leg. Put the soles of your feet together.
- Take turns pushing your foot forward and backward.
- Return to the starting position.
- Repeat the exercise with the other leg.

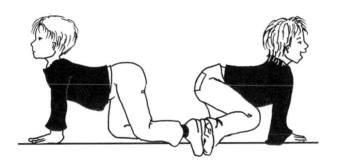

91 Turn on Your Axis

- Sit facing each other with legs spread apart and feet touching.
- One raises the right leg, and the other raises the left leg, and you roll over on your stomachs.
- Keep your feet in contact and rise up in the Downward-Facing Dog pose (Exercise #62).
- Walk your hands toward your feet and raise yourself with buttocks touching.
- Stand back to back with your eyes closed for a moment or two.

- Return to the starting position.
- Repeat the sequence a few times.

92 Sitting Twist

- Sit cross-legged, facing each other.
- Place your right arm behind your back and take each other's left hand.
- Breathe in, twist away from your partner, and look behind you over your right shoulder.
- Breathe out and turn forward again.
- Repeat a few times.
- Return to the starting position.
- Repeat the sequence, changing hands.

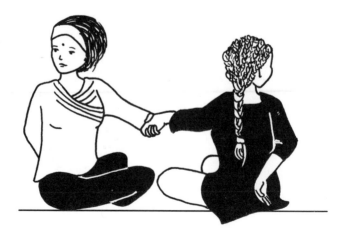

93 Standing Twist

- Stand up straight back to back and hold hands.
- Breathe in and bring your arms up in the air.
- Breathe out and bend to one side.
- Breathe in and stand up straight again.
- Breathe out and bend to the other side.
- Repeat the sequence several times.

94 Bending and Stretching

- Stand up back to back with legs apart.
- Breathe in, raise your arms outward and up, and stretch them above your heads.
- Breathe out and bend forward from the hips.
- Grab each other's hands between your legs.
- Hold this position and breathe gently.
- Let go of each other's hands, breathe in, and stand up slowly.
- Repeat the sequence several times.

95 Arm Lift

- Sit on the ground, one behind the other.
- The one in front puts her hands together behind her back.
- The one behind catches hold of the other's hands and raises the arms gently.
- The one in front should indicate when to stop.
- Lower the arms again slowly.
- Repeat the exercise and then change places.

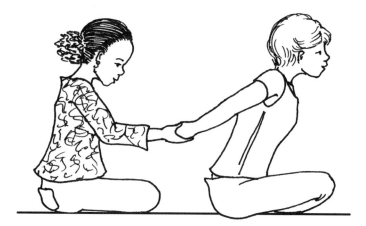

96 Pyramid

- Sit on the floor, facing each other.
- Bend your legs and put the soles of your feet on those of your partner. Take each other's hands outside your legs.
- Stretch the legs upward to form a pyramid, with your hands keeping you balanced.
- Hold this position and then return to the starting position.

- Repeat the sequence, but this time hold your hands on the inside and raise your legs outside the arms.
- Repeat the sequence several times.

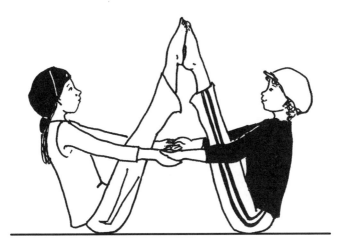

97 Trees

- Stand side by side with shoulders touching.
- Place your weight on your inside leg.
- Bend the outer leg and place your foot on the inside of your other thigh.
- With your inner hand, grasp your partner's foot.
- Bring your other arm behind you and take your partner's hand.
- Hold this position and try to keep your back as straight as you can.
- Return to the starting position.
- Repeat the exercise but change places so you use the other leg.

98 Turtles

- Sit on the ground back to back.
- Draw up your legs and put your feet flat on the floor.
- Sit up by shifting your weight to your feet and then reach your arms backward through your legs and take your partner's hands.
- Carefully lean over forward until your head touches the ground.
- Breathe evenly and hold the posture for as long as you comfortably can.
- Return to the starting position.
- Repeat the sequence several times.

99 Rowing

- Sit facing each other with legs spread apart.
- Place your soles together and take your partner's left hand in your left hand.
- As one breathes out, bending forward, the other breathes in and bends back.

- Then the other breathes out, bending forward while the other breathes in and bends back.
- Repeat the sequence several times.

100 Up and Down

- Sit on the ground back to back.
- Draw up your legs and place your feet flat on the floor.
- Link arms and push your feet into the floor.
- Breathe in, stretch your legs, and rise up together.
- Breathe out and sink back to the floor.
- Repeat the sequence several times.

101 Plows

- Lie on your backs head to head, with the tops of your heads just touching.

- Stretch your arms sideways and slightly upward to hold hands.

- One partner breathes in, raising his legs over his head and letting them down carefully to touch the other's navel.

- As he breathes out, he brings the legs back over and down to the ground.

- Change places and repeat the sequence.

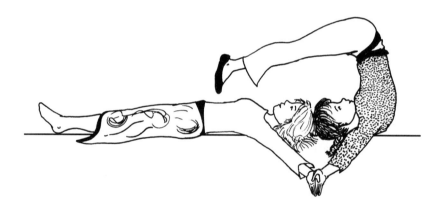

Visualizations
and Waking Up

The Language
of the Elements

In this part of the book, students will make a journey through the elements earth, water, air, and fire. They will be taken on a magical imaginary adventure. By becoming aware of their thoughts, teens can break through the limitations of reality so that their powers of imagination will increase and they will find more of an emotional balance.

Remind your students that the elements earth, water, air, and fire can help them become more aware of their bodies. The element earth gives physical power and stability. The element water helps mobility and the ability to solve problems. The fluid nature of water helps feelings and wishes flow along. Air is the bond between the inner and outer worlds and conducts the flow of your moods and emotions in and out. When you see and recognize the things around you, it puts you in a lighthearted mood. The element of fire gives you the energy to make the right choice and to focus on your goals. By directing your attention within and trying to experience the corresponding element in yourself, you can increase your powers of perception. Look to see how close you are to yourself (earth), what moves you (water), how much energy you have (fire) and how consciously you are living your life (air).

With the aid of the following visualization exercises young people will be able to concentrate on mental pictures in order to create a particular feeling; for instance, letting go of stress and the commotion of the day. A well-developed capacity for visualization can be a great help to teens in school with such subjects as history and geography. It can also help them prepare for exams.

A journey through the elements takes young people on an adventure to quiet, safe places that they can create in their own minds. Each story is different, but the message is always the same: Let go of stress and the hustle and bustle of the day.

The journeys will capture your students' imaginations even better if you play soft music combined with the sounds of nature. When reading the story, pause in between sentences. As the story approaches its end, the students take leave of the place to which they have traveled, breathe more deeply, move their fingers and toes, and finally open their eyes. Afterward they can make drawings of the journey. The exercises serve not only to increase the capacity for imagination, but it can also help the participants learn to use their senses more consciously.

102 Earth

- Start by lying on your back.
- Close your eyes.
- Breathe in and out gently.
- With each breath, your body becomes heavier and heavier.
- You are standing in the forest with a huge mountain before you.
- You admire the mountain for its power and immovability.
- Imagine that you are the mountain.
- Feel stronger, more solid, and strongly rooted.
- Your body becomes more and more grounded in the earth.
- The sun rises and shines down on you.
- Gradually you become warmer and warmer.
- The forest around you comes to life.
- The birds fly around you and land in the treetops.

- Listen to the sounds around you. (Pause 5 minutes.)
- Your body is powerful, and you are in complete balance.
- You have complete trust in your own power.
- Rain begins to fall on you. You glisten.
- It is spring, summer, fall, winter.
- Days and nights become longer and then shorter.
- You remain unchanged, strong and stable.
- You enjoy the peace within yourself and the peace surrounding you… (Pause 5–10 minutes.)
- The sun goes down.
- It becomes colder and colder.
- It is time to leave the mountain.

103 Water

- Start by lying on your back.
- Close your eyes.
- Breathe in and out gently.
- With each breath, your body becomes heavier and heavier.
- You are lying on the beach on a beautiful summer day.
- Smell the sharp sea air.
- Feel the breeze softly touching your cheeks.
- Relax your eyes…your mouth…your jaw….
- The tide is rising. The water is coming closer and closer to you.
- The surf is tickling your toes.
- It is delightfully calm and warm.
- Now the water is touching the rest of your body.
- You are drifting on your back in the water.

- You are gently carried back and forth on the waves.
- Take a look under the water.
- As you look around, you can see schools of fish in all colors of the rainbow.
- The colors move as the sun glitters on them.
- You become aware of how quiet it is under the water.
- Breathe in and feel how relaxed your body is becoming.
- Breathe out and feel the tension flowing out of your body.
- Let your feelings and wishes stream along with the water.
- Your mind is quiet.
- Be aware of how relaxed you become within yourself as the tension drains away.
- Enjoy the pleasure of the silence... (Pause 5–10 minutes.)
- It is time to leave.
- Swim back to the shore.
- The warmth of the sun dries your body.

104 Air

- Start by lying on your back.
- Close your eyes.
- Breathe in and out gently.
- You are lying in the garden.
- It is a lovely summer day.
- The sky is a beautiful blue.
- There are clouds in all shapes and sizes, changing constantly.
- Your body is becoming lighter and lighter.
- Imagine that you are slowly floating upward.

- A soft breeze carries you higher.
- You flap your arms, carrying yourself higher.
- Enjoy the wonderful feeling of flying.
- You see all kinds of birds as you fly upward.
- Look down and see how small everything on earth has become.
- Now you are right up among the clouds.
- As you fly, your body has become completely relaxed.
- Feel your feet…your legs…your arms…your hands…your stomach…your shoulders…and your face.
- All the tension in your body flies away with the wind.
- You have all the time you want to explore the environment around you. Or you can stay where you are and look at all the possibilities you have while you are as free as a bird. (Pause 5–10 minutes.)
- It is time to leave again.
- Fly back home.

105 Fire

- Start by lying on your back.
- Close your eyes.
- Breathe in and out gently.
- It is a warm day.
- The sun is glowing red in the sky.
- The sun warms your body.
- Your face is warm, and now you feel the sun on your arms, your stomach, your legs….
- Your whole body is now wonderfully warm.
- Enjoy the warmth and feel your connection with the sun.
- You are on the brink of making important choices in your life.

- The sun gives you the energy to find clarity and helps you make those choices.

- The rays of the sun caress you, and the heat relaxes your body.

- Continue to enjoy the ability to choose and the energy that the sun gives you. (Pause 5–10 minutes.)

- It is time to leave the sun.

Waking Up

After coming out of the visualization exercise and wiggling your fingers and toes, it is nice to try one of the following exercises.

106 Close to Yourself

- Lie down on your back.
- Draw your knees up and place your feet flat on the floor.
- Cross your arms over your chest.
- Feel how your back makes more contact with the floor.
- Lie there, breathing gently in and out.

107 Tail Wagging

- Lie down on your back.
- Draw your knees up to your chest.
- Put your hands under your head and lift your head up.
- Move your whole body quickly to the left and the right.
- Stop the exercise and stretch your legs.
- Open your eyes and slowly come into a sitting position.

108 Walking on Air

- Lie down on your back.
- As you breathe in, lift your left hand and your right leg.
- Your soles and palms are pointing upward toward the ceiling.
- Breathe out and lower your arm and leg back to the floor.
- As you breathe in, lift your right hand and left leg.
- Repeat the exercise several times.
- Stop and stretch your legs.
- Open your eyes and slowly come into a sitting position.

109 Wringing

- Lie down on your back.
- Draw up your knees and place the soles of your feet together.
- Put your palms together.
- Rub your hands and feet together.
- Do this for a few minutes.
- Stretch your legs, close your eyes, and put your hands on your eyes.
- Feel the warmth of your hands on your eyes.
- Stop and stretch your legs.
- Open your eyes and slowly come into a sitting position.

110 Circles on Your Back

- Lie down on your back.
- Draw your knees up and grasp them with your hands.
- Rock yourself to the left and to the right (with a slight circular motion) as though massaging your back against the floor.
- Return to the starting position.

111 Swinging

- Lie down on your back.
- Bring your legs up above your stomach.
- Cross your legs and take your right foot in your left hand and your left foot in your right hand.
- Rock backward and forward a few times.
- Sit up cross-legged.
- Rock a few times to the left and right from the Tailor pose (Exercise #51).

The **Exercises Arranged** by **Specific Categories**

Advanced Exercises

Exercises Requiring a Mat

Exercises Requiring a Large Space

Exercises Requiring Musical Accompaniment

Exercises in Which Physical Contact Might Be Involved